SQUADRONS!

No. 11

THE NORTH AMERICAN
MUSTANG MK. IV
OVER ITALY AND THE BALKANS

PHIL H. LISTEMANN

ISBN: 978-2918590-80-4

Copyright

© 2015 Philedition - Phil Listemann

Revised August 2019, June 2021, March 2022, September 2024

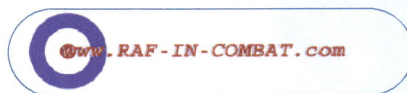

Colour profiles: Gaetan Marie/Bravo Bravo Aviation

GLOSSARY OF TERMS

PERSONEL :

(AUS)/RAF: Australian serving in the RAF
(BEL)/RAF: Belgian serving in the RAF
(CAN)/RAF: Canadian serving in the RAF
(CZ)/RAF: Czechoslovak serving in the RAF
(NFL)/RAF: Newfoundlander serving in the RAF
(NL)/RAF: Dutch serving in the RAF
(NZ)/RAF: New Zealander serving in the RAF
(POL)/RAF: Pole serving in the RAF
(RHO)/RAF: Rhodesian serving in the RAF
(SA)/RAF: South African serving in the RAF
(US)/RAF - RCAF : American serving in the RAF or RCAF

RANKS

G/C : Group Captain
W/C : Wing Commander
S/L : Squadron Leader
F/L : Flight Lieutenant
F/O : Flying Officer
P/O : Pilot Officer
W/O : Warrant Officer
F/Sgt : Flight Sergeant
Sgt : Sergeant
Cpl : Corporal
LAC : Leading Aircraftman

OTHER

ATA: Air Transport Auxiliary
CO : Commander
DFC : Distinguished Flying Cross
DFM : Distinguished Flying Medal
DSO : Distinguished Service Order
Eva. : Evaded
ORB : Operational Record Book
OTU : Operational Training Unit
PoW : Prisoner of War
PAF: Polish Air Force
RAF : Royal Air Force
RAAF : Royal Australian Air Force
RCAF : Royal Canadian Air Force
RNZAF : Royal New Zealand Air Force
SAAF : South African Air Force
s/d: Shot down
Sqn : Squadron
† : Killed

CODENAMES - OFFENSIVE OPERATIONS - FIGHTER COMMAND

CIRCUS:
Bombers heavily escorted by fighters, the purpose being to bring enemy fighters into combat.

RAMROD:
Bombers escorted by fighters, the primary aim being to destroy a target.

RANGER:
Large formation freelance intrusion over enemy territory with aim of wearing down enemy fighters.

RHUBARD:
Freelance fighter sortie against targets of opportunity.

RODEO:
A fighter sweep without bombers.

SWEEP:
An offensive flight by fighters designed to draw up and clear the enemy from the sky.

THE MUSTANG MK. IV

The North American Mustang belongs to the category of the legendary fighters of WWII. The Mustang IV was the British version of the USAAF P-51D that was introduced during the spring of 1944. This version had the new cockpit canopy that was highly appreciated by the pilots. This one-piece moulded Perspex sliding hood provided very good visibility in the most important direction – rearwards. Another improvement was the armament that increased from four 0.5-in machine guns in the Mustang Mk.III to six in the Mk.IV. A derivative was also put in production, the P-51K, which differed only in the type of propeller fitted. The latter became the Mustang IVA in the RAF inventory. The RAF had long wanted the Mustang for its units based in England, the Middle East and the Far East but, as priority was given to the USAAF Fighter Groups, it was not until very late in 1944 that these new Mustangs were released to the RAF.

The British received two Mustang P-51Ds (**TK586** and **TK589**) from USAAF stock for evaluation in July 1944. They were from the very first batches, Block Five, and were formerly 44-13524 and 44-13332. The British took delivery between September 1944 and January 1945 of thirty Mustang Mk.IVs, with serials **KH641 to KH670** (ex 44-11168 to 11187 and 44-11253 to 11262), and 200 Mustang Mk.IVAs, with serials **KH671 to KH870** (ex 44-11374 to 11413 and 44-11478 to 11517). This was the balance of the 450 Mustang III previously ordered but only the first 220 were delivered as Mk.IIIs. These Mk.IVs were diverted from the North American Aviation plant in Dallas, Texas, and all were Block Five models. The Mk.IVAs built at the same plants were diverted from Block One (80) and Block Five (120). One of these, KH660, crashed before delivery at its home base of Dallas on 23 August 1944. It crashed during a test flight and its pilot, First Lieutenant Joseph W. Garard, was killed.

The first Mustang IVs to be introduced into RAF inventory were TK586 and TK589 in June 1944 (for testing). Below: 44-13332, still with its USAAF serial, later changed to TK589. Both were former P-51D-5s built at Inglewood in California and would the only RAF Mustangs built at the original North American plant. The rest of the RAF's Mustang IV and IVA supply would be built at the North American plant at Dallas, Texas. Up to the P-51D-20, the Mustang was mainly used as a fighter while from the P-51D-25 its fighter-bomber capabilities were improved with the introduction of underwing hardpoints for five-inch rockets or two 500 or 1,000-lb bombs. *(Phil Butler)*

MUSTANG IV
PACKARD MERLIN
JUNE 1944

Another view of 44-13332 (TK589) at Boscombe Down. *(Phil Butler)*

Later on the British could order, via Lend-Lease, another batch of 900 Mustang Mk.IV/Mk.IVAs was ordered and delivered in the sequence after the last Mustang from the previous batch. The serials allocated were **KM100 to KM492** for 392 Mustang Mk.IVAs (172 Block Ten and 181 Block Fifteen, 44-11953 to 11858, 44-12263 to 12433, 44-12552 to 12602, 44-12628 to 12707 and 44-12759 to 12809) and **KM493 to KM743** for the 251 Mustang Mk IVs (all Block Twenty, 44-12903 to 12942, 44-12960 to 12999, 44-13050 to 13100, 44-13141 to 13180, 44-13221 to 13252, 44-84391 to 84397, 44-84468, 44-84681 to 84720) delivered until August 1945 when Lend-Lease was terminated. Consequently, the last 56 Mustang IVs (KM744 to KM799) were not delivered and were never shipped to the UK and the balance KM744 to KM999 never built. A further five crashed before delivery. KH689 was later repaired and repossessed by the US. KH839 was lost on a ferry flight within the USA on 10 December 1944 and the same thing happened with KM419 (7 March 1945), KM425 (2 March 1945, its pilot, Flight Officer William A. Quinn was killed) and KM486 (22 March 1945). In all, 869 Mustang Mk.IVs/IVAs were taken on charge by the RAF.

Of those that reached their destination, the UK-based squadrons were the first to take the new Mustang on strength. About 550 were sent to the UK, followed by about 100 for the Mediterranean and then 225 were shipped to the Far East. In the Mediterranean area, including after the war, six RAF squadrons (93, 112, 213, 249, 250 and 260), three SAAF squadrons (1, 2 and 5) and one RAAF squadron (3) used the Mustang Mk.IV as part of the Balkan Air Force. They were flown, in conjunction with the older Mk.IIIs, on fighter-bomber missions. The Mk.III was progressively retired in favour of the newer Mk.IV and the later aircraft remained the only mark used after the war for the squadrons that remained operational until 1947. Within Fighter Command, nine squadrons were fully equipped with the Mk.IV (19, 64, 65, 122, 126, 154, 234, 303 (Polish) and 611) for escort duties before the war ended. No. 154 Squadron was, however, disbanded in March 1945. By VE-Day fifty Mustang Mk.IVs had been struck off charge for various reasons and the Mustang IV continued to serve for a short time. As Lend-Lease terminated in September, all spare parts had to be paid for so the Mustang withdrawal was set, and the squadrons were either disbanded (1 and 2 SAAF in July, 249, 260, 611 and 3 RAAF in August 1945, 5 SAAF in October 1945, 303 in November 1946, 93, 112 and 250 in December 1946), or converted onto British-made aircraft (122 and 234 to Spitfire Mk.IXs in August 1945, 19 and 65 to Spitfire XVIs on March 1946 and May 1946 respectively, 64 to Hornets in May 1946 and 213 to Tempest VIs in February 1947). The Americans, having plenty of Mustangs in various storage facilities, did not ask for the aircraft back and all were scrapped in situ before 1947 ended.

Compared to the US, the usage of the North American P-51D was relatively negligible with about 3500 sorties flown during the war, two-thirds in the Miditerranean, and few claims made. The main reason for this is that the mark was introduced late in the war, the Americans having supplied their units first, but the Mustang Mk.IV would have played a major role in the RAF had the war against Japan lasted longer. It is worth noting that the RAF was not the only beneficiary of the release of large numbers of P-51D/K in 1945 as the RAAF, RNZAF and NEIAF were all in the process of either converting their units or receiving deliveries of the aircraft.

As far as the MAAF (Mediterranean Allied Air Forces) is concerned, the following serials were initially allocated to this theatre (but transfers were made later on like KH682 or KH741):

Mk. IV: None.

Mk. IVA: KH671, KH677, KH679, KH681, KH684, KH692, KH693, KH699, KH701, KH705-706, KH710, KH716-717, KH723, KH731, KH736, KH740, KH745, KH755, KH776, KH771-806, KH808-810, KH813-817, KH820-821, KH823-824, KH827-828, KH830-832, KH837, KH842, KH846, KH851-852, KH856, KH861, KM104-105, KM107, KM117, KM119, KM127, KM135-136. *(72)*

As far as the Far East is concerned, the following serials were allocated to this theatre:

Mk. IV: KM525, KM538, KM541, KM543, KM545, KM548-549, KM553-554, KM557, KM562, KM564, KM569, KM573-574, KM576, KM577, KM582, KM584-587, KM589-591, KM593, KM595, KM597, KM600-601, KM604-743. *(170)*

Mk. IVA: KM147, KM154, KM169, KM174, KM385, KM438, KM478. *(7)*

KH802 was built as a P-51K-5-NT (44-11710) and earmarked for the Mediterranean area where it was photographed at an unrecorded location. The P-51K was a P-51D with an Aeroproducts propeller instead of the usual Hamilton Standard unit. The Aeroproducts propeller was generally not preferred by most US crew chiefs and many props were not balanced well. Originally ordered on 21 July 1943, 1,500 P-51Ks were produced and one third went to the RAF. The production was split into four blocks. The K-10 was the most produced with 600 being built (172 went to the RAF). It was this block that introduced the underwing hardpoints for five-inch rockets or two bombs. In US service more than 150 P-51Ks were converted to a reconnaissance fighter configuration as F-6Ks while the rest were mainly used in the CBI or Pacific theatres. KH802 seems not to have served in any operational unit but, as many records were destroyed after the war, nothing can be certain except that it was struck off charge in January 1947. It would be the fate of the surviving Mustangs which were scrapped when not needed by the Americans. *(Phil Butler)*

KH828, another Mustang IVA built as a P-51K-5-NT (44-11736), seen during a test flight. This aircraft was issued to No. 5 Squadron SAAF in January 1945. Stored when the squadron returned to the Union in October 1945, it was struck off charge in March 1946. The Mediterranean theatre actually received a small number of Mustang IVs compared to the Western Europe and Far East theatres. This can be explained by the fact that the Mediterranean was not a major theatre by the end of 1944 while the Luftwaffe was still seen as a threat in Western Europe and the re-conquest of Malaya and the invasion of Japan was, of course, a major issue. Also, the attrition of Mustang Mk. IIIs in the Med was below expectations so there was a lower priority to replace losses and withdraw the last Kittyhawks. But, against all odds, it would be in the Med that the Mustang IV would be used most intensively. After November 1944, the Mustangs left the factory in a natural metal finish. Only the first Mustang IVs were painted and it is worth noting that the colours used - Olive Drab, Sea Grey and Light Grey - were US paint colours.

SUMMARY OF THE OPERATIONAL ACTIVITY OF THE MUSTANG III & IV IN ITALY 1944-45*

Squadron	Type	Sorties	Total per Sqn	Claims	Op. Losses	Acc. Losses	Losses
3 Sqn RAAF	Mk III	975		-	11	-	
	Mk IV	800	1,775	2.0	6	-	17
5 Sqn SAAF	Mk III	1,350		-	24	-	
	Mk IV	870	2,220	2.0	8	1	33
112 Sqn	Mk III	3,520		1.0	26	1	
	Mk IV	530	4,050	-	4	6	37
213 Sqn	Mk III	2,060		23.66	42	1	
	Mk IV	300	2,360	-	9	3	55
249 Sqn	Mk III	1,350		1.0	24	-	
	Mk IV	-	1,350	-	-	-	24
260 Sqn	Mk III	4,810		-	26	1	-
	Mk IV	-	4,810	-	-	-	27
Grand Total			16,565	31.66	180	13	193

* up to 30.09.45

Victories - confirmed or probable claims: 2.0

First operational sortie:	Number of sorties: *ca.*800
02.12.44	**Total aircraft written-off: 6**
Last operational sortie:	
05.05.45	Aircraft lost on operations: 6
	Aircraft lost in accidents: -

Squadron code letters:

CV

COMMANDING OFFICERS

S/L Murray P. NASH	AUS. 400101	RAAF	...	08.03.45
F/L Kenneth A. RICHARDS (*Temp.*)	AUS. 400104	RAAF	08.03.45	03.05.45
S/L Murray P. NASH	AUS. 400101	RAAF	03.05.45	...

SQUADRON USAGE

No. 3 Squadron, RAAF, was a long-serving fighter unit in the Mediterranean when the first Mustangs arrived in November 1944. It had been equipped with Gladiators, Hurricanes, Tomahawks and, for the preceding two years, all marks of Kittyhawks had seen service. From May 1944, the squadron was equipped with the Mk.IV for ground attack duties. The squadron was based at Fano in Italy and had been commanded by S/L Murray P. Nash from the end of October. Nash had served with the squadron for more than a year and had been awarded the DFC and Bar.

The Kittyhawk had been regarded as obsolete by the RAF for a long time but in Italy, where the air opposition was almost non-existent, the Kittyhawk soldiered on and excelled in the ground attack role. However, from the second half of 1944, a replacement for the type had become a necessity and, consequently, the squadron received its first Mustang Mk.III in mid-November. The squadron was rested for only five days to complete the transition on to the new type and the first operation was mounted on the 22nd. At that time, only one Mk.IV was on charge, KH677/CV-P (later recoded ◊), and this became the CO's mount. He first used this Mustang to lead the squadron on a fighter-bomber sortie, to attack marshalling yards at Bjelovar in Yugoslavia, on 2 December. The operation lasted three hours and all aircraft returned to base. Four more ops were led by the CO in his Mk.IV. During these he claimed three M/T destroyed, three more probably destroyed, and three damaged, and also damaged a locomotive. In the meantime, more Mk.IVs had been issued - KH679/CV-G, taken by one of the flight commanders, F/L J.A.T. Hodgkinson, and KH716/CV-P

Two long-serving members of No. 3 Squadron and two DFC & Bar holders. Left, Murray Nash, who arrived in January 1943 and commanded the squadron twice (until April 1944 and from October 1944 for his second tour). Ken Richards, right, completed two tours with the squadron - the first between August 1943 and October 1944 and the second from February 1945 onwards. He was awarded the DFC in March 1944.

Murray Percival NASH
AUS. 400101

Enlisting in May 1940, Murray Nash, from Victoria, Australia, served for two years as a flying instructor before being posted overseas at the end of 1942. In January 1943, he joined No. 3 Squadron RAAF, located in North Africa at that time, flying Curtiss Kittyhawks. He opened his score soon afterwards by claiming the probable destruction of a Bf109 over Tunisia on 7 March 1943. He shared the destruction of an Italian SM79 four days later.

Following the progression of the squadron to the European continent, he continued to participate in the numerous ground-attack operations the squadron was tasked with, becoming a flight commander in October. This led to the award of the DFC in March 1944, soon followed by a Bar in July 1944. In the meantime, he had been promoted to command the squadron in February until the end of his tour in April. In October 1944 he returned to the squadron to lead it a second time. During this time he made his last claim, a Bf109 damaged, to bring his total to one shared confirmed victory, one probable and one shared damaged aircraft. He temporarily left the squadron in March to attend a Fighter Leader's course in the UK, returning two months later, and continued to lead the unit until August when the squadron was repatriated. He received the DSO that same month. He left the service in December 1945.

North American Mustang Mk IVA KH716
No. 3 Squadron, RAAF
Squadron Leader MP Nash
Fano (Italy), winter 1944-1945

A well-known photograph of a mixed flight of Mustang Mk IIIs and IVs of 3 Sqn presuming returning from a raid over northern Italy. The first three aircraft are in bare metal while the last two have been camouflaged in dark green and medium sea grey. The closest aircraft, a Mk IVA (KH853/CV-K), was usually piloted by F/L Ken Richards who had chosen the individual letter to correspond to the initial of his first name. This photo was actually taken during the summer of 1945 which explains why the aircraft are not carrying ordnance. Note the distinctive Southern Cross design (white stars on a blue background) on the rudders of the aircraft. This was unique to 3 Sqn and an extravagance that was accepted with the end of the war approaching. *(AHM of WA)*

which became soon the new CO's mount. Ground attack missions continued during the month as usual but something unusual occurred on the 26th when the formation, led by the CO and attacking a railway, was surprised by two Bf109s. They shot down one Mustang Mk.III whose pilot, W/O Quinn, was able to bail out. The CO ordered bombs to be jettisoned and turned to attack the two German fighters. They were able to escape but one was damaged by S/L Nash, in his Mk.IV, and two other pilots flying Mk.IIIs. This was the first claim by any Mk.IV in this theatre. In a way, this attack was a success for the Germans as one Mustang was destroyed and the attack on the railway was prevented.

In January 1945, the squadron was still operating over Yugoslavia, with some intrusions in to northern Italy and Austria, with little opposition to report. Flak was the main danger but, depending on the targets, it ranged from light to intense with the latter being rarely encountered at this stage of the war. Each Mustang was usually equipped with two 500-lb bombs. Despite bad weather in January preventing any flying for a third of the month, the squadron was able to carry out close to 230 sorties. The Mk.IV counted for 25 per cent of these flights and the new arrivals were KH710/CV-E and KH821/CV-Y. The latter would have a short career as it was lost on 25 January during an attack on a railway. The formation of twelve aircraft had just reformed after a dive-bombing attack on a bridge and was looking for other targets to attack when F/O Davies called up to say that he had engine trouble. Davies was ordered to return to base escorted by three other Mustangs. However, he could not make it and was forced to ditch his aircraft with a dead engine. He was picked up by a Walrus that had taken off after the first emergency warning.

Mustang KH760/CV-Z, was painted with the standard RAF camouflage (actually with US paints). It is seen here loaded with two 500-lb bombs under the wings, the classic load for fighter-bomber missions. This Mustang became operational in mid-April 1945 and was usually flown by F/O Ian G.S. Purssey, from Queensland, who would continue to serve in the RAAF after the war. *(AHM of WA)*

Mustang KH794/CV-G at dispersal at Cervia in Italy in March or April 1945. It was usually flown by F/O Allen F. Shannon, from New South Wales, who had also served with No. 450 (RAAF) Squadron in 1943 (an Australian unit which was still equipped with Kittyhawks). One of 450's aircraft can be seen in the background. With this aircraft he would make the squadron's last, an Fi156, claim on 3 April. *(AHM of WA)*

In February, F/L John A.T. Hodgkinson assumed temporary command from the 12th as S/L Nash attended a Fighter Leader course at Tangmere in the UK. February was similar to January but the squadron only flew for half of the month as bad weather was either encountered over the aerodrome or over the target. The number of Mk.IVs increased during the month as many Mk.IIIs had to be progressively sent to MU for overhaul or major repairs that were beyond the squadron's capabilities. The new comers were KH723/CV-K, KH806/CV-L and KH851/CV-Y. That month the squadron also carried out various escorts to No. 250 Squadron's Kittyhawks. It was like a breath of fresh air for the pilots to fly escort operations. More than 180 sorties were flown in February, a third by Mk.IVs, and no losses were sustained. The number of Mk.IVs increased during the month as many Mk.IIIs had to be progressively sent to MU for overhaul or major repairs that were beyond the squadron's capabilities. The Mk.IIIs, therefore, were mostly replaced by brand new Mk.IVs. Hence, by the beginning of March, about half of the Mustangs on strength were Mk.IVs.

March, contrary to the two previous months, was very intense. Losses remained light, with the squadron losing its first on the 3rd. Fortunately, the pilot of the Mk.III managed to bail out. On the 7th, F/L Hodgkinson, who was temporary in charge of the squadron, took off to lead a formation of twelve Mustangs (including seven Mk.IVs as the pilots mostly preferred flying a Mk.IV instead of a Mk.III) to attack flak positions around a bridge near Padua. Over the target the formation split off to attack the various German positions in a diving attack. After having bombed one of the positions, F/L Hodgkinson was heard to call up and say that he had been hit and was therefore making for home. The other pilots saw black smoke streaming from his aircraft as he headed south at high speed. He managed to climb to 5,000 feet as two Mustangs of the squadron arrived as escort. However, after a little while, things worsened and the black smoke intensified and was soon followed by white smoke that indicated the glycol coolant was leaking. Hodgkinson had no option but to bail out and was seen reaching the ground safely while his Mustang, KH679/CV-G, exploded upon hitting the ground. He spent the last weeks of the war as a PoW. The next day, F/L K.A. Richards, a long-serving member of the squadron, took command on the orders of the CO of No. 234 Wing, G/C Eaton, an Australian, while the flight commander position, vacated by the temporary loss of Hodgkinson, was taken over by F/O A.F. Shannon who began his second tour in February.

He had completed his first tour with the squadron and No. 450 (RAAF) Squadron. The rest of month was occupied with carrying out ground attack sorties although, in the second half of the month, the squadron was called on several times to escort Marauders attacking targets in southern Austria. For March, the Mustang IV flew half of the 460 sorties carried out which indicated that the Mk.IV was continuing to replace the now ageing Mk.III within the unit. March saw the arrival of KH755/CV-W, KH794/CV-G, KH830/CV-T, KH831 and KH866.

April would become the busiest month of the Mustang era with more than 700 sorties carried out. Half of these were made by Mk.IVs. The Allies wanted to precipitate the end of the war in Italy and continued to pressure the Germans who now retreated on all fronts. This strategy would have a cost, however, with the squadron losing no less than seven Mustangs in the process (three were Mk.IVs). April did not begin well with one Mustang IV lost on the first day of the month when it was hit by flak while attacking a target in Yugoslavia during an armed reconnaissance early in the day. Hit at 50 feet, the pilot, F/L D.B. Davies, was able to climb to 4,000 feet, streaming smoke. He was seen to jettison his hood, bail out and land safely on the ground before disappearing into the woods 100 yards away. The next day the loss of KH851 was compensated by the claim made by F/O A.F. Lane, who, during another armed reconnaissance in the first hours of the day, encountered a Fieseler Fi156 Storch. The formation of four Mustang IVs found a column of vehicles and, as they attacked, Lane saw the Fi156 flying at 2,000 feet. He wasted no time in catching the Fi156 and then fired at it from astern. The German pilot was unable to escape and chose to make a forced landing. The Fieseler was then strafed by Lane and, with back-up from F/L Edmonds, who was leading the operation, the aircraft was set on fire while the German crew made their escape. The next day, two operations were flown, one in the early hours of the morning, where various vehicles were claimed as destroyed or damaged, and another one at midday consisting of six Mk.IIIs and only two Mk.IVs. This op started out very well when, while flying over enemy-held territory looking for targets of opportunity, another Storch was seen at 50 feet flying below the formation. Flight Lieutenant A.F. Shannon, flying a Mk.IV, and his wingman jettisoned their bombs to intercept the nimble liaison aircraft. Shannon made a full beam attack from starboard and hit the Fieseler in the engine and cockpit. The German aircraft was seen smoking and then dived to the ground where it crashed in flames. The mission continued and eventually targets of opportunity were found and many claims made. The Germans had their revenge, however, by shooting down two Mk.IIIs. Both pilots succeeded in bailing out. After months of relative quietness, the squadron had shot down two German aircraft in two days but had lost three Mustangs including one Mk.IV. On 11 April, the squadron made five Cab-rank patrols (each of three aircraft). The second one took off at 1335 and was led by an RAF pilot, F/L 'Jungle Jim' Edmonds, who had recently been attached to the squadron. He was the only one flying a Mk.IV. The target was three guns reported to be hidden in a yard. The three aircraft dive-bombed the yard and saw a big explosion despite having seen no flak around. When pulling out, Edmonds' wingmen, W/Os T.R. Higgins and P.J. Martin, realised the explosion had been caused by their leader's Mustang. Even today, there is no clear explanation as to what caused him to dive into the ground but it is believed he blacked out during the dive. Edmonds would become the last 3 Squadron pilot to be killed during the war.

Bad luck continued, however, when, on 16 April, twelve Mustangs, including five Mk.IVs, took off at 1525 loaded with bombs to attack a motorised unit HQ near Bologna. However, W/O Wells encountered engine trouble just after take-off and was forced to

Mustang KH755/CV-W was among the aircraft not allocated to any pilots and was flown by various Warrant Officers including W/O Lewis R. Ranger and W/O Donald S. Williamson. The latter had to make an emergency landing on 29 April 1945. Note the letter 'W' painted on the gear door. In the hands of F/O Lane, however, it was earlier used to destroy an Fi156 on 2 April. *(AHM of WA)*

Mustang IV KH716 seen at Fano with two 1,000-lb bombs under the wings. This aircraft, left in a natural metal finish, would become Nash's favorite aircraft and when he left for the Fighter Leader Course in March 1945 this Mustang naturally became the new mount of Ken Richards (who would use KH853/CV-K later on, see previous page). Note the serial left as it was painted at the factory. This was a very common sight in this theatre while in the UK all were repainted under the stabilisers. *(AHM of WA)*

return to base where he crash landed alongside the strip with the bombs still on the wings of KH710. The squadron continued to harass the enemy troops and before the month was over would lose two more Mustangs including one Mk.IV, KH755, on 29 April. That day, the squadron, for the third operation of the day, sent six aircraft with all but one being Mk.IVs. It was an armed recce over the north-east of Italy. Led by F/L Shannon, the formation eventually found a convoy that they attacked at once. They bombed and strafed and three vehicles were claimed as destroyed and others as damaged. The formation then reached the coast where a loaded barge was also strafed. Then, coming out over the coast at 4,000 feet, the Mustang of W/O Williamson was seen streaming glycol and, of course, began to overheat. Without waiting any longer, he decided to make an emergency landing and did so successfully off Venice. During the month, Mustang IVs KH723/CV-W, KH732, KH735, KH749, KH760/CV-Z, KH772/CV-Z, KH786/CV-C, KH807/CV-Y, KH845/CV-B and KM104/CV-J had arrived to make-up for attrition.

In May the war finally ended but, even though the Germans surrendered on the 2nd, operations were still flown and about fifty sorties were carried out (35 of them were on Mk.IVs). The last attack was carried out on 1 May and was an anti-shipping mission led by F/O I.G.S. Purssey early in the day. Some more recces were flown to locate pockets of Germans but no more attacks were required. The last recce, a flight over the Trieste-Fiume area, was recorded on 5 May. When the twelve aircraft led by F/O B.L. Burton landed at 1550, the war was over for the squadron which had logged close to 800 sorties on Mk.IVs. The following weeks were mainly spent preparing for repatriation and in August, after five years of overseas service, the personnel left for Naples to embark for Australia.

Claims - 3 Squadron, RAAF (Confirmed and Probable)

Date	Pilot	SN	Origin	Type	Serial	Code	Nb	Cat.
02.04.45	F/O Alan F. LANE	AUS. 409150	RAAF	Fi156	KH755	CV-W	1.0	C
03.04.45	F/L Allen F. SHANNON	AUS. 412715	RAAF	Fi156	KH794	CV-G	1.0	C

Total: 2.0

Four pilots of No. 3 Squadron RAAF, operating in northern Italy in close support of the Eighth Army, pose in front of a Mustang IV at the end of the war. Left to right: F/O Ian G. Purssey, W/O John B. Taylor from New South Wales, F/O B. L. Burton from New South Wales and F/L Alan F. Lane, of Queensland, who made one of the squadron's last two claims of the war.

Summary of the aircraft lost on Operations - 3 Squadron, RAAF

Date	Pilot	S/N	Origin	Serial	Code	Fate
25.01.45	F/O David B. DAVIES	AUS. 406924	RAAF	KH821	CV-Y	-
07.03.45	F/L John A.T. HODGKINSON	AUS. 411495	RAAF	KH679	CV-G	PoW
01.04.45	F/O David B. DAVIES	AUS. 406924	RAAF	KH851	CV-Y	-
11.04.45	F/L James T. EDMONDS	RAF No. 114755	RAF	KH677	CV-◇	†
16.04.45	W/O Donald J. WELLS	AUS. 406924	RAAF	KH710	CV-E	-
29.04.45	F/L Allen F. SHANNON	AUS. 412715	RAAF	KH755	CV-W	-

Total: 6

Above, Mustang KH676/CV-A was issued to the squadron at the end of the hostilities and was usually flown by Alan Lane. *(via Drew Harrison)*
Below KH830/CV-T in the postwar lineup at Lavariano. The ghost of the 'D17' code it wore with 5 RFU can be seen where the '7' had been removed among with part of the serial that it crossed. The others in the lineup are KH760/CV-Z, KH819/CV-X, FB295/CV-W (a Mk III), HB955/CV-L (a Mk III) and KH690/CV-P with its distinctive camouflaged rudder. *(AHM of WA)*

Victories - confirmed or probable claims: *nil*

First operational sortie: 04.12.44	**Number of sorties:** *ca.*870
Last operational sortie: 03.05.45	**Total aircraft written-off:** 9

Aircraft lost on operations: 8
Aircraft lost in accidents: 1

Squadron code letters:
GL

COMMANDING OFFICERS

Maj David W. MURDOCH	SAAF No. 205706	SAAF	...	20.03.45
Maj Hendrick O.M. ODENDAAL *(Eva.)*	SAAF No. 103164	SAAF	20.03.45	03.04.45
Maj Hillary J.E. CLARKE *(†)*	SAAF No. 21685	SAAF	03.04.45	01.05.45
Capt Alan Q. DE WETT *(Temp.)*	SAAF No. 48142	SAAF	01.05.45	20.05.45
Maj Hendrick O.M. ODENDAAL	SAAF No. 103164	SAAF	20.05.45	15.10.45

SQUADRON USAGE

Under the authority of the RAF from the end of 1941, No. 5 Squadron SAAF fought over the Western Desert, and then Italy, flying Tomahawks and Kittyhawks before being re-equipped with the Mustang Mk.III in September 1944 to continue the fighter-bomber role. For the final months of 1944 the pilots were operating ahead of the 8th Army whose advance had finally been halted by heavy rains, snow and mud. In December 1944 the squadron was based at Fano and was under the command of Maj. David 'Dave' Murdoch who had the distinction of being one of the very few Allied pilots to have shot down an Fw190 while flying a Kittyhawk.

As the squadron was entering its fourth year of continuous operations, the first of the Mk.IVs (KH736) arrived. This aircraft flew operationally for the first time on the 4th on an armed reconnaissance led by Capt. Clarke over the Brod-Sarajevo area. Two days

Lt James H. McD Davidson posing on one the very first Mustang IVs taken on charge by the squadron. As he left during the first days of December 1944, being tour-expired, this Mustang is probably KH736, the first IV issued to the squadron.
(M. Schoeman)

Hendrik Oswald Meyer ODENDAAL

SAAF No. 103164

'Tank' Odendaal enlisted in January 1940 and, upon completing his training, served in South Africa as a flight instructor during the first years of the war. In July 1943 he volunteered to serve up north in the Desert Air Force and attended No. 73 OTU in August and September. His first assignment was to deliver aircraft at No. 3 ADU, a posting he retained until November. At the end of December, after a short refresher course at No. 239 Wing Training Flight, he was posted to No. 5 Squadron SAAF as a captain and took over a flight commander position. The squadron, based in Italy, was flying the Kittyhawk IV that had recently been introduced into the RAF. He left in June 1944 as tour expired and was awarded the DFC in September. He returned to the Union and instructed again. In January 1945 he was back with No. 5 Squadron, as a flight commander once again, and was finally given command of the unit at the end of March. However, two weeks later, he was shot down by ground fire in Mustang IV KH805/GL-V, but managed to evade capture, rejoining the squadron on 12 May. He added a Bar to his DFC in July and continued to command the unit until October when he was sent back to the Union. 'Tank' Odendaal continued to serve in the SAAF after the war, participating in the Korean War in 1950 and receiving a US DFC in 1954. He eventually retired from active service in June 1976 as a Brigadier-General.

North American Mustang Mk IVA KH805
No. 5 Squadron, SAAF
Captain HOM Odendaal
Cervia (Italy), March 1945

North American Mustang Mk IVA KH805
No. 5 Squadron, SAAF
Major HOM Odendaal
Lavariano (Italy), summer 1945

later the same aircraft was flown by Capt. William B. 'Bill' Lombard, a long serving member of the squadron, on another armed reconnaissance, at the head of a formation of eight other aircraft. Heavy clouds were met on the way across the Adriatic. The Mustangs were still flying over cloud two hours later. Captain 'Bill' Lombard ordered the pilots to descend to get under the clouds. The formation started to lose cohesion as they did so. While some were turning for home, Blue section tried to follow Lombard's section. Blue section quickly lost sight of Lombard but he was heard on the radio getting a course from Highfield control. That would be the last thing ever heard of him. He became the first Commonwealth pilot to be killed flying a Mk.IV in Italy but his loss was not the only one sustained by the squadron as six Mustang IIIs, and three pilots, were lost in the same circumstances. The squadron had lost almost half of its fighting force in a single operation. Replacement aircraft soon arrived to replace these losses (KH681 and KH692 and KH740). KH740 would have a very short career with the squadron as it was lost in an accident during a test flight on the 13th. The engine failed during the take off run and the pilot, Capt. Enslin, had to make an emergency stop which ended badly for the aircraft. Enslin escaped injury however. The two other Mk.IVs were sent on operations for the first time on the 11th, for KH692 with Capt Clarke on an armed reconnaissance, and on the 15th for KH681 when Capt. Peter G. MacGuire, B Flight Commander, flew it and led a cab-rank of six Mustangs (four Mk.IIIs). A cab-rank mission was a fighter-bomber patrol maintained over the front lines to be called down upon targets by RAF liaison officers embedded with forward elements of the Army. Usually the Mustangs carried two 500-lb bombs under the wings. This first mission lasted less than two hours and the formation returned to base at 10.00 after attacking tanks west of Faenza. No claims were made. Shortly after midday, MacGuire took off again to lead another cab-rank mission, being the only one flying a Mk.IV this time. Other Mk.IVs were introduced in the following days. KH717 was first sent on operations with Lt Robert G. 'Ossie' Osler on the 22nd and was flown by the CO on the 28th as he led a strafing mission while carrying a single 1000-lb bomb. The squadron flew just over 200 sorties during December 1944. Twenty-two of them were flown by the three Mk.IVs the unit had on strength.

Mustang IV KH681/GL-Z was one the first Mk. IVs used by the squadron and was the Mustang Capt Peter MacGuire, from Durban, was flying when he was killed on 4 February 1945 as OC of B Flight. He had joined the squadron in June 1944. The South Africans used to repaint the red of the national markings in orange. This was done within several days of the aircraft's arrival. (M. Schoeman)

When KH805 arrived at the squadron in February 1945, it was not long before it became the regular mount of Capt 'Oddie' Odendaal. He kept it when he took command of the squadron and was shot down in this aircraft. He successfully evaded capture - see colour profile.
(S. Bouwer)

In January, the squadron continued operations as it had left off. A fourth Mk.IV was added to the inventory, KH731, and was first flown by Capt. Hillary 'Nobby' Clarke, the other flight commander, on the 10th for an attack on railway tracks. KH808 and KH828 had also arrived by the end of the month. The Mk.IV was now the expected replacement for the Mk.IIIs lost on operations or withdrawn for overhaul. This was welcomed by the pilots who quickly realised the value of the improved visibility the Mk.IV's 'bubble' canopy provided. This explains why, of the 188 sorties flown that month, 44 were by the Mk.IVs despite the small number on the squadron. By the end of January the squadron had five Mk.IVs on hand as KH717 had been lost on the 23rd. That day, the squadron had been called up to attack a railway bridge and the formation, comprising ten Mustangs (including two Mk.IVs), took off at 10.20. The target was identified and attacked and many direct hits were recorded. However, this attack was not one-sided as two aircraft failed to return. KH717, flown by Capt. Barney 'Geoff' Enslin, was seen to catch fire while diving but the crash was not seen. Enslin, from Pretoria, was on his second tour of operations and had joined the squadron in October.

The squadron only lost one Mk.IV on operations in February. Unfortunately, it also lost its B Flight CO, Capt. MacGuire. He was shot down on the very first operation of the month, on the 4th, when he was leading an attack on a rail bridge and was seen to crash between two houses. MacGuire, from Durban, had joined the squadron in June 1944 as a Lieutenant and eventually took command of B Flight during the autumn. Due to widespread bad weather that prevailed over the area in February, the squadron was only able to fly 154 sorties, of which half were flown by Mk.IVs, but nearly all of the sorties employed 1,000-lb bombs. The aircraft on hand at the end of the month were KH692, KH731, KH800, KH805, KH808, KH813, KH817 and KH828. The Mk.IVs now made up half of the squadron's inventory.

With the war in Italy accelerating towards a conclusion, the squadron concentrated its attacks on roads and railways that by this stage were becoming the way for German troops to retreat towards the Alps and the Austrian border. On 23 February the squadron moved a short distance north and took up station at Cervia near Rimini. It would remain there until the end of the war. March was a busy and successful month for the squadron. More than 460 sorties were carried out, 300 of them by Mk.IVs, and 380 1000-lb bombs and 452 500-lb bombs were dropped (includes figures for the Mk.III). The high sortie count for the Mk.IVs was indicative of there being only four Mk.IIIs remaining on strength (KH705, KH796, KH799, KH810 and KM105 were added during the month and KH731 departed). As March came to a close, most of the sorties were flown by Mk.IVs as the squadron was keen to be the first to be totally equipped with the new mark. By mid-March, a big change occurred when Maj. 'Dave' Murdoch relinquished command to Capt. Hendrik O.M. 'Oodie' Odendaal who had been awarded the DFC during his previous tour with the squadron. Odendaal had started another tour in January. A logical step actually as 'Oodie' Odendaal was leading the squadron in operations since the beginning of the month. While March can be seen as a successful month with no loss to report, April would be totally different. Operations continued over northern Italy and Yugoslavia. Within two days, two Mustang IVs were lost on operations. On 2 April, the squadron was sent for the second mission of the day, an armed recce over Maribor-Leibnitz. Around Leibnitz, the South Africans saw the roads blocked with transport vehicles. The Mustangs attacked in two groups, each one selecting a part of the road. The bombing attack was followed by strafing runs and many scores were recorded on cars, transports and concentrations of horses and carts. However, the troops on the ground were far from inactive and ground fire encountered was accurate enough to hit the aircraft (KH705) flown by Lt. Donald Boyd. He bailed out and would become a PoW until released six weeks later. Boyd had previously completed a tour with the squadron while flying Tomahawks over Tobruk and had rejoined in December 1944 for his second tour. The next day the CO led the squadron twice but did not return from the second operation. The task of the day was to destroy a bridge in northern Italy. The first attempt in the morning failed because of the weather so the squadron had to return in the afternoon. The formation split up after crossing the coast with Odendaal leading Red section. Coming down to bomb more than 200 rail trucks in the marshalling yards at Celje, his Mustang (KH805) was seen to be hit by flak and he was observed to bail out. His parachute opened successfully and he landed among trees that hid him from view. Odendaal managed to evade capture but did not return until after the end of the war in May. In the meantime he was replaced by Capt. 'Nobby' Clarke who had been awarded the DFC in mid-March and had a tally of three confirmed victories on Kittyhawks while serving with the squadron in 1943-1944 over Tunisia and Italy. After a bad start, April improved over the next fortnight despite intense activity. Indeed, the squadron carried out about 250 sorties during that time, mainly with the Mk.IVs. This luck eventually came to an end on 17 April when Lt. 'Roy' Sleep was seen to crash near a road south-east of Brescia while strafing vehicles during the first mission of the day. The day was not over as two 'Rover Paddy' cab-ranks followed at 06.35 and 07.10 then, at 11.25, now Major Clarke led eleven Mustangs (half being Mk.IVs) to bomb a bridge. Only near misses were scored but the intense and accurate flak damaged three aircraft (including KH807 flown by Lt. Neville J.E. Mathee). The CO, flying KH692, suddenly found his cockpit full of hot Glycol and oil. He jettisoned the cockpit hood and was able to return to base safely even though his undercarriage dropped from lack of hydraulic pressure. Two days later, the squadron lost Capt. Johannes 'Jan' Coetzee during a ground attack mission shortly after midday. When attacking, he called that he had been hit and would try to make base. He didn't make it. His No. 2, Lt Albert Ibsch saw Coetzee's Mustang catch fire and spiral into the ground. The pilot was not seen to bail out. Coetzee had served since 1941 with Nos. 43, 4, 1 and 2 Squadrons of the SAAF for his first tour and had been serving with the squadron since the previous September. A DFC would be gazetted in July 1945. Besides the losses sustained by the Mk.IVs, the squadron lost two other pilots on Mk.IIIs on the 17th and 23rd, both killed in action, then, on the 24th, Lt. 'Jack' Filby was killed in action during the first mission of the day. His Mustang KH808, which was flying straight and level, suddenly hit the ground while strafing, bounced, and turned over before bursting into flames about sixteen miles west of Padua. He had either lost control or was hit by ground fire. The exact cause could not be determined. The next day the squadron almost lost another Mustang IV when KH810, flown by Capt. Alan Q. de Wet, suffered engine damage from 20mm flak shells but fortunately made it home. Other Mk.IVs were damaged by flak in the following days. KH798 (Capt. Royer C. Lever) was hit on the 26th and again on the 28th with the same pilot as were KH817 (Lt. Mathee) and KH796 (Lt. Jozua J. Kruger). The Germans still had plenty of fight. All that made for an intense but deadly month for the squadron which completed 573 sorties, 396 on Mk.IVs, and dropped ten 1000-lb bombs and 834 500-pounders. Despite the losses, the squadron could count on twelve Mk.IVs (KH671/GL-N, KH673, KH692/GL-D, KH741/GL-I, KH753, KH768, KH796, KH810, KH813, KH814, KH826, KH828) but the

Mustang IV KH692/GL-D was Clarke's regular mount and he was flying this aircraft on his final and fateful mission of 1 May 1945. Note the 1,000-lb bomb under each wing. (M. Schoeman)

17

Hillary John Ellis CLARKE
SAAF No. 21685

'Nobby' Clarke enlisted in the SAAF in June 1940. Upon completion of his training in April 1942, he was first posted to No. 10 Squadron, SAAF, then under formation in South Africa for home defence duties. The unit's Mohawks were soon replaced by Kittyhawks. He remained with this unit until December 1942 and joined No. 3 Squadron in North Africa flying Hurricanes one month later. He was soon re-posted to No. 5 Squadron SAAF, to fly Kittyhawks. He fought over Tunisia during the last weeks of the campaign and made his first two claims - a Ju52 on 19 April 1943 and an Me323 three days later. Following the squadron as it advanced into Sicily and Italy, he became a flight commander and returned to the Union at the end of his tour in April 1944. He had made his last claim, a twin-engine German aircraft, two weeks earlier on the 6th to bring his total to three confirmed victories.

He returned to operations in October 1944 to serve once more with 5 Squadron which had converted to Mustangs a couple of weeks before. He flew many operations over the Balkans and Italy and received a DFC in March 1945. The next month he was given command of the squadron but was sadly shot down in his Mustang, while engaged in the squadron's last operation of the war, on 1 May 1945. Clarke was the last SAAF pilot killed in action during WW2.

North American Mustang Mk IVA KH692
No. 5 Squadron, SAAF
Major HJE Clarke
Cervia (Italy), April-May 1945

losses sustained by the Mk.IVs prevented the squadron from being totally equipped with the type so several Mk.IIIs remained on strength at the end of April.

On the first day of May the squadron mounted its final series of operations. In the morning it was called to attack gharries near Udine (six aircraft led by Capt. de Wet). Another op, led by Capt. Roland P.J. Woolcott , was also flown but, as with the previous one, no target was attacked. Both formations returned to base after having jettisoned their bombs into the sea. In the afternoon the CO led the squadron on the last mission of the day, a shipping strike between Trieste and Grado. When the Mustangs reformed, the CO was not among them. It was presumed that he had been shot down by flak. This was confirmed by pilots of No. 112 Squadron who reported seeing an explosion on the coast and a pall of black smoke. Clarke was the fourth CO to be lost in action since the squadron went to war and would be also the last SAAF pilot to be killed in action during WW2. De Wet would act as OC until the return of Odendaal who would command the squadron from 20 May until disbandment on 15 October 1945 at Lavariano (Udine) where the squadron moved to on 10 May. On 2 May Axis forces in Italy were surrounded but the squadron continued to fly. It first flew an ASR mission in the hope of finding the CO before flying two more cab-rank missions. A final mission was carried out on the 3rd when six MK.IVs, led by Lt. Basil J.R. Creasey, took off at 11.55 and flew over the now quiet Trieste and Fiume area. The six Mustangs returned at 14.00 and the war for the squadron was over, and the squadron would return to the Union in October, after having moved to Lavariano on 10 May as temporary peacetime station. With 33 sorties completed in May, the squadron had carried out a total of 867 sorties on the Mk.IV since its introduction. This was the highest number of sorties on this type flown by a Commonwealth squadron during WW2.

Date	Pilot	S/N	Origin	Serial	Code	Fate
23.01.45	Capt Barney G.S. ENSLIN	SAAF No. 47311	SAAF	KH717		†
04.02.45	Capt Peter G. MacGuire	SAAF No. 103825	SAAF	KH681	GL-Z	†
02.04.45	Lt Donald N. BOYD	SAAF No. 205567	SAAF	KH705		PoW
03.04.45	Maj Hendrik O.M. ODENDAAL	SAAF No. 103164	SAAF	KH805	GL-V	Eva.
17.04.45	Lt Royston SLEEP	SAAF No. 542777	SAAF	KM105		†
19.04.45	Capt Johannes C. COETZEE	SAAF No. 103385	SAAF	KH713		†
24.04.45	Lt Jack E. FILBY	SAAF No. 42988	SAAF	KH808	GL-E	†
01.05.45	Maj Hillary J.E. CLARKE	SAAF No. 21685	SAAF	KH692	GL-D	†

Total: 8

Mustang IV KH808/GL-E in which Lt Filby lost his life on 24 April 1945. It was not his regular mount, however, but Capt A.Q. de Wet's as seen here seated in KH808. *(M. Schoeman)*

Date	Pilot	S/N	Origin	Serial	Code	Fate
13.12.44	Capt Barney G.S. ENSLIN	SAAF No. 47311	SAAF	KH740		-

Total: 1

Victories - confirmed or probable claims: -

First operational sortie: 03.12.44	**Number of sorties:** *ca.* **535**
Last operational sortie: 05.05.45	**Total aircraft written-off: 12**

Aircraft lost on operations: 4
Aircraft lost in accidents: 8

Squadron code letters:
GA

COMMANDING OFFICERS

S/L Anthony P.Q. BLUETT	RAF No. 43539	RAF	...	19.03.45
S/L George L. USHER *(eva.)*	RAF No. 88251	RAF	19.03.45	20.03.45
F/L Paul M. FORSTER *(Temp.)*	RAF No. 106650	RAF	20.03.45	04.04.45
S/L John S. HART	RAF No. 41696	(CAN)/RAF	04.04.45	19.10.45
S/L Peter S. BLOMFIELD	RAF No. 47767	RAF	23.10.45	04.12.45
S/L Paul M. FORSTER	RAF No. 106650	RAF	04.12.45	29.04.46
S/L Maurice J. WRIGHT	RAF No. 117704	RAF	02.05.46	29.11.46
S/L Reginald T. LLEWELLYN	RAF No. 47380	RAF	29.11.46	31.12.46

SQUADRON USAGE

No. 112 Squadron converted to the Mustang III in July 1944. It was stationed at Cervia in Italy when the first Mk.IV arrived. The CO, S/L A.P.Q. Bluett, was a very experienced pilot who had flown in the Mediterranean area for a long time having previously served with 6 Squadron, on Hurricanes, where he had been awarded the DFC. The first Mk.IV to be taken on charge was KH701/GA-Q at the end of November 1944. It flew its first operation with F/L Ray V. Hearn in command. Another experienced pilot, he had been the B Flight commander since July when he started his second tour. He had received the DFC and Bar. That day, he led seven Mk.IIIs on a ground attack operation in the Treviso area. The formation was recalled off Venice, however, while landing back at base the new Mustang stalled on approach short of the runway and collided with a previously crashed Liberator. The Mustang still had its two bombs under the wings but they, fortunately for the pilot and the immediate surroundings, did not explode.

Squadron Leader Bluett, left, posing with Lt Paul, SAAF. Bluett began his first tour with 6 Sqn, and was awarded the DFC, before being posted to 112 Sqn in May 1943 as OC A Flight. Posted out for a rest in March 1944, he returned to the squadron in July 1944 and remained with it until March 1945. A Bar to his DFC was awarded at the same time. Lieutenant Dennis Paul, arrived in November 1944 for his first tour. He was repatriated to the Union in July 1945.

Mustang IVA KH774/GA-S in flight. The photo was probably taken after the end of the war as the aircraft is not carrying any ordnance or an auxiliary fuel tank. This Mustang was taken on squadron charge in April 1945 and was usually flown by South African Lt Dennis G. Paul.

The bombs were actually the main cause of the stall as the aircraft was much heavier than usual on approach, something the pilot was now only too aware of. The squadron remained without a Mk.IV during the next few weeks before receiving KH820 which was also coded GA-Q. Its first operation was carried out on 8 February and was again flown by Hearn. He was leading four Mustang IIIs (two others returned early) to attack the Dobrava marshalling yards. It was the first op for a couple of days as the weather had grounded the aircraft. The six Mustangs returned to base in pairs with Hearn returning with his wingman, Sgt Ralph B. Robinson, two and a half hours later. Until the 17th, no further operations were carried out owing to bad weather but sorties resumed that day when twelve aircraft were detailed to attack a rail diversion at Venzone in northern Italy. Only one Mk.IV was part of the formation, KH852/GA-P, recently taken on charge, and flown by F/L Paul M. Forster (the A Flight CO). The mission was executed without anything special to report. The next day, after an early weather reconnaissance over Yugoslavia, the squadron dispatched eight aircraft over northern Italy near Dogana, where the weather was more favorable, where a viaduct had to be destroyed. Led by F/L Hearn in KH820, the only Mk.IV in the formation, the viaduct was attacked before Hearn headed to Aviano airfield for a strafing run. Sadly, his machine was hit by flak and set on fire. Hearn climbed to 2,000 feet by which time the Mustang was engulfed in flames with pieces dropping off. The aircraft then entered a flat spin and was seen to explode on the ground with no sign of a parachute. In the meantime, other Mk.IVs had arrived at the squadron: KH793/GA-L (first flown on operations by Capt. Grahame W. Schwikkard SAAF on the 20th) and KH824/GA-V (which became the CO's machine from 21 February onwards). By the end of the month other Mk.IVs were introduced to operations - KH795/GA-Y, KH824/GA-V and KH852/GA-P. The squadron ended the month with four operational Mustang Mk.IVs. Less than 150 sorties were completed in February with only nineteen being flown by Mk.IVs. Bad weather had prevented most of the planned operations, especially during the first fortnight, and, furthermore, poor results were recorded for the ground attack operations that had been carried out.

In March the squadron continued its operations with a mixed force of Mk.IIIs and Mk.IVs with the majority still being the Mk.III. Only 150 sorties, of a total close to 500, were flown by Mk.IVs. All missions were ground attack support, against a great variety of targets, over Yugoslavia and northern Italy. Despite this number of sorties flown, only a Mk.III on the 11th and a Mk.IV on the 20th (KH793/GA-L) were lost. By mid-March, it was known that the CO, S/L Bluett, would leave the squadron by the end of the month. His position would be taken over by the B Flight commander, F/L 'Laury' Usher, who had begun his third tour in September the year before. Bluett had let Usher lead the squadron, to help ease the transition, before Usher took command of the Squadron on 19th. However, the next day his command came to an end when he was shot down during an attack on the Ljubljana marshalling yards during the first mission of the day. The six aircraft started with a recce of the Trieste-Ljubljana rail line and then attacked the marshalling yards causing considerable damage to buildings and trains. They then took another heading and, near Kranj, the formation strafed another train when Usher's machine was seen streaming glycol after probably being hit by flak. He was seen to pull away and bail out. He was left hanging in his harness from a tree with locals hurrying towards him. He would return to the squadron later on. Being tour expired, Bluett did not continue to command the squadron however. Squadron Leader John S. Hart, a Canadian serving with the RAF and a veteran of the Battle of Britain, who had been previously posted in as a supernumerary Squadron

22

Leader, took over 4 April, replacing F/L Paul Forster, the temporary CO. He became CO when Bluett left on 4 April with a new DFC ribbon on his chest. For the record, Usher was also among the pilots who received the DFC in March. At the end of the month the number of Mk.IVs had increased to eight with KH776/GA-?, KH795 (recoded GA-G), KH824/GA-V, KH832/GA-J, KH852/GA-P, KM107/GA-M, KM135/GA-K and KM136/GA-B on strength.

In April, more than 580 sorties were carried out. The Mk.IVs flew 335 which proves the number of Mk.IVs had increased markedly since March. However, this number was soon reduced by one when, on 2 April, F/L Maurice N. Matthias, a native of Kenya and the new B Flight commander, was killed in KM135/GA-K while leading four aircraft (including two Mk.IVs leading each section) on an armed recce to Ljubljana, Radeče, Celje, Pragersko, Maribor, and Ptuj where some captive balloons were seen over the marshalling yards. North of the rail line, locos and other targets were seen and attacked from 8,000 to 1,500 feet. Two MTs and one direct hit on a road was recorded. At that time, two aircraft returned to base owing to engine trouble but Matthias continued the mission with his wingman, the South African Eric J.G. 'China' Gauntlet, to the north of Graz. South of the town, targets were seen and duly attacked but Matthias' Mustang was hit in the Glycol tank while flying at only 200 feet. He climbed to 1,500 feet and began a glide but stalled. A parachute appeared briefly at about 400 feet after the hood had been jettisoned but the aircraft dived into the forest and caught fire. Matthias had been posted to the squadron in February 1945 for a second tour after having served his first tour with 112 between 1943 and 1944. It was a bad day for the squadron as it lost another pilot in a Mustang III. The unit was kept busy over the next few days but no losses were reported. On the 12th, more than thirty sorties were flown but two aircraft were lost. Flight Sergeant T.P. Roberts, in KM127/GA-X (received a couple of days before), failed to return, the other being a Mustang III - KH571. He was observed to pull out after the attack but was not seen again. He had been with the squadron for only about three weeks. The squadron would lose another Mk.III before the end of the month but, in any case, the war was close to its end at that time. Alongside KM127/GA-X, received that month and already lost, other Mk.IVs were added to the inventory: KH734/GA-B (replacing KM136), KH763/GA-F, KH774/GA-S, KH862/GA-X and KH872/GA-? (KH776 being recoded GA-K).

In May a couple of sorties were flown, the last ones on 6 May. All were on Mk.IVs and two recces were flown with one in the morning (Lts Ellis F. Blatchford and William O. Davenport SAAF) and one in the late afternoon (Lt Blatchford again and F/Sgt Robinson). When the last pair landed at 19.35, the war was over for the squadron. However, sadness would continue to visit 112 in the following weeks. As early as 13 May, Sgt P.L. Greaves, who had been missing since January and returned on the 2nd, was killed while flying at 3,000 feet in a practice formation off Forli. His engine failed and, instead of bailing out, he attempted a forced landing. The aircraft turned over as it hit some trees and the young pilot had no chance to escape. A couple of days later the squadron moved to Lavariano and would stay there for the next ten months. On 20 July, while returning from a cross-country, the starboard undercarriage of KH719, flown by Capt. Gordon 'Eddie' Edwards SAAF, jammed half way and, after various attempts to lower the leg, the pilot decided to bale out. He did so successfully and saw his Mustang disintegrate upon hitting the ground. The worst was still to come for

A line-up of 112 Squadon's Mustang IVs in May 1945, the nearest being KH832/GA-J. After VE-Day, flights would become sporadic in autumn mainly due to a lack of difficult to procure spares. (*ww2images.com*)

Date	Pilot	S/N	Origin	Serial	Code	Fate
18.02.45	F/L Raymond V. HEARN	RAF No. 102547	RAF	KH820	GA-Q	†
20.03.45	S/L George L. USHER	RAF No. 88251	RAF	KH795	GA-Y	Eva.
02.04.45	F/L Maurice N. MATTHIAS	RAF No. 119867	RAF	KM135	GA-K	†
12.04.45	F/Sgt Thomas P. ROBERTS	RAF No. 1623387	RAF	KM127	GA-X	†

Total: 4

the squadron. On 26 July, or 'Black Thursday' as it would be known, nine aircraft took off at 9.55, led by Capt. Edwards, for a practice recce. Of these, two had to return to base owing to engine trouble. They were the lucky ones. The rest of the formation continued and a strafing exercise began in a valley somewhere between Trento and Lake Iseo. The formation then re-formed in line astern and set course along a valley under cloud. After only a few seconds, two of the pilots, Lt Andries van Aardt (SAAF) and Sgt Klibanski, realised that this was not an open-ended valley and that cloud covered the mountains that lay directly ahead. Van Aardt immediately stall-turned his machine and miraculously escaped hitting the mountainside while Klibanski, from Palestine, opened up full throttle, climbed as hard as he could and missed the mountaintop by only a few feet. Behind him he saw a series of explosions in the cloud and none of the five other pilots survived (all but one in a Mk.IV). Of the pilots who were killed, four were South Africans and, sadly, very close to being repatriated home. Therefore, in a couple of weeks, the squadron's composition changed with all of the Dominion personnel leaving along with the last Mk.III still on strength. The squadron stayed at Lavariano until March 1946 when it moved to Tissano. A couple of weeks before, on 27 November, another death was recorded when Sgt Headland was killed in KM271 after possibly having suffered from oxygen starvation. Seven months later, the starboard tyre of KH773 burst on landing and the aircraft swung off the runway and nosed over on uneven ground, damaging the undercarriage and mainplane but the pilot, F/O I.G Probert escaped injuries. The Mustang was not repaired and that would be become the last accident sustained by the 112 on Mustang. Another move took place in September to Treviso. This was the squadron's last station before it disbanded on 31 December.

Date	Pilot	S/N	Origin	Serial	Code	Fate
13.05.45	Sgt Peter L. GREAVES	RAF No. 1808528	RAF	KH763	GA-F	†
20.07.45	Capt Gordon H. EDWARDS	SAAF No. 11208	SAAF	KH719		-
26.07.45	Capt Gordon H. EDWARDS	SAAF No. 11208	SAAF	KM216		†
	Lt Raymond H. TEMPLER	SAAF No. 581465	SAAF	KM107	GA-M	†
	Lt Ronald D. PARK	SAAF No. 543052	SAAF	KH720		†
	Lt Wreford D. BLOM	SAAF No. 581737	SAAF	KM235		†
27.11.45	Sgt Albert E. HEADLAND	RAF No. 1584911	RAF	KM271		†
19.06.46	F/O Ivor G. PROBERT	RAF No. 163311	RAF	KH773		-

Total: 8

John Stuart HART

RAF No. 41696

A Canadian, John Hart travelled to the UK and joined the RAF on a short-service commission in January 1939. In October 1939, his training complete, he was posted to No. 1 School of Army Co-operation and, during the summer of 1940, flew Lysanders with Nos. 614 and 613 Squadrons.

When, during the Battle of Britain, Fighter Command called for volunteers, Hart stepped forward and undertook a Spitfire conversion in August. In September, he was posted to No. 54 Squadron but was almost immediately posted to No. 602 (City of Glasgow) Squadron. He opened his score on 12 October by sharing in the destruction of a Ju88. Other claims followed in the ensuing weeks. In March 1941, he moved to No. 91 (Nigeria) Squadron where he made his last claim on 28 April to bring his tally to three confirmed victories (two shared) and one damaged. In July, he became a flight commander, a position he held until the end of his tour in October.

Volunteering to serve overseas, Hart was sent to the Far East in August 1942, joining No. 79 (Madras Presidency) Squadron in February 1943. In May, he was given command of No. 67 Squadron. His tenure was brief, however, as he was given a staff position in July. He returned to operations in June 1943 as supernumerary squadron leader but was again posted away in September 1944 to No. 73 OTU in Egypt until April 1945 when he took command of No. 112 Squadron in Italy. He left 112 in August with a DFC previously received in June.

North American Mustang Mk IVA KH774
No. 112 Squadron
Cervia (Italy), April 1945

Victories - confirmed or probable claims: -

First operational sortie:
06.02.45

Last operational sortie:
05.05.45

Number of sorties: 299

Total aircraft written-off: 17

Aircraft lost on operations: 9
Aircraft lost in accidents: 8

Squadron code letters:
AK

COMMANDING OFFICERS

S/L Peter E. VAUGHAN-FOWLER	RAF No. 110008	RAF	...	17.01.46
S/L Raymond S. NASH	RAF No. 119808	RAF	17.01.46	04.11.46
S/L Maurice C. WELLS	RAF No. 37535	RAF	04.11.46	02.01.47
S/L Denis C. COLEBROOK	RAF No. 40890	RAF	02.01.47	...

SQUADRON USAGE

Under the leadership of S/L Peter E. Vaughan-Fowler (who had distinguished himself while serving with No. 161 (Special Duties) Squadron) from November 1944, No. 213 Squadron was already familiar with the Mustang having flown the Mk.III since May 1944. When the first Mk.IV arrived at the squadron, to reinforce the Mk.IIIs, the unit was located at Biferno in Italy. The squadron began to receive the Mk.IV in February 1945 but only in very small numbers. Mustang KH794 was the first to be used on operations on the 6th, for a weather recce flown by F/O Frederick A.E. Person, leading a Mk.III flown by W/O Peter M. A. Johnston. The latter took the opportunity to strafe and disable a loco while the Mk.IV held its fire. Actually, the 6th was not the first day a Mk.IV flew with the unit as the day before G/C Ducan S. MacDonald (who led the 213 in 1940 - 1941), in KH706, had flown with the squadron. On the 7th, KH794 was in Australian F/L Frederick M. Gamble's hands for another weather recce with a Mk.III. Gamble was the first to fire a squadron Mk.IV's guns in anger and opened the type's account with three trucks claimed destroyed and four more damaged. During the next day KH794 was only used for weather recce. The only offensive operation carried out was alongside KH706 (G/C MacDonald). KH794 was usually flown by the CO. It was not until the 12th that a second Mk.IV was used on operations (KH671). On the 14th the two Mk.IVs flew together for the first time with the CO in KH671 leading F/O Peter Donnelly for an armed recce during which rail traffic was strafed and many targets hit and damaged. On the way back they flew over Brege landing ground and here the CO strafed and damaged a Ju52 parked among trees on the southern perimeter. Those two sorties were actually the last for twelve days as the two Mk.IVs left the squadron and were replaced by others. During that period of time KH693, KH803, KH809, KH823, KH826, KH846 and KH861 were added to the inventory and, naturally, they were immediately used, carrying out half of the sorties flown on the 28th.

On 1 March various sweeps were launched around the Zagreb area. The two marks on strength did not fly mixed formations where possible. Three Mk.IVs took off at 07.35, led by F/O Arthur G.R. Ashley, for a tactical recce as movement had been reported during the night. Nothing, however, was seen. Just north of Zagreb, Ashley said on the R/T that he was low on fuel and was flying on his last tank. He told his two wingmen, F/Os 'Jack' Donnelly and Don E. Robertson (RNZAF), to continue and that he would try to make it back to Zara. However, it became clear to Ashley that the twenty gallons remaining in the tank would not be enough to reach Zara and that he would have to bail out of KH823. He reported the situation to Donnelly and Ashley and jettisoned the canopy. After some initial trouble, he succeeded to getting out of his diving Mustang. Upon reaching the ground, he was saved by a group of partisans and was happy to be back with the squadron in a couple of days. Bad luck continued, however, for the pilots flying Mk.IVs as the next day another one was lost on operations (KH846). F/O Donnelly was listed as missing during a weather recce. He had taken off at 06.35 as No.2 to F/L Gamble (RAAF) for this mission. During the flight they found some targets to attack and

Peter Erskine VAUGHAN-FOWLER
RAF No. 110008

Peter Vaughan-Fowler enlisted in the RAF in the autumn 1940. In November 1941 he completed his training and was posted early in 1942 to No 161 (SD) Squadron with a commission. Recently formed, this unit mainly equipped with Westland Lysanders was to fly insertion missions at night into occupied France, and had the role of delivering SOE agents, wireless operators, wireless equipment and weapons to assist the resistance. He eventually left 161 in September 1943, being posted for a short time to 21 Squadron flying Mosquitoes. During the year, he had been awarded a DFC in April and a Bar was added in leaving the squadron.

In February 1944, another tour started in the same role but in Italy with No 148 Squadron, taking a flight commander position until August. After a short conversion course on Mustang, he was posted to No 213 Squadron in November to command, a position he kept well after the end of war. In August, he was made Companion of the DSO. He served with the RAF after the war.

North American Mustang Mk IVA KH861
No. 213 Squadron
Biferno (Italy), June 1945

A group of 213 Sqn's pilots posing proudly around Mustang IV KH861, one of the first Mk. IVs issued to the squadron. Note that the squadron code letters seem to be yellow outlined in black. KH861 is sometimes reported to have been lost on 1 March but after two weeks of absence it seems to have returned to service. It had probably been repaired during this time. *(D.E Robertson via Paul Sortehaug)*

strafed vehicles along the main road leading north out of Zagreb. As Gamble was about to attack a bus, he saw women jumping out and decided to abort the attack and told Donnelly to do the same. Donnelly acknowledged the call but, just one minute later, Gamble lost sight of him. The R/T remained silent and Gamble landed back at base at 09.25. What happened to Donnelly was discovered much later. He was actually hit by heavy machine gun fire and was obliged to bail out about forty miles west of Zagreb. He tried to evade capture but was eventually captured by the Ustashi, handed over to the Germans and sent to a PoW camp in Germany. During the next few days, bad weather, a persistent shortage of aircraft (the squadron having an average of less than eight aircraft available on a daily basis) and the long distance from Biferno to the main areas combined to reduce the number of operations but not the losses. On the 11th, two more Mustangs were lost. One of these was a Mk.IV lost to ground fire and if its pilot, W/O Ian R.H. Iago, was able to bail out, he was too low for his parachute to open completely before he hit the water. Despite an ASR launch arriving on scene, no trace of him could be found. New Mk.IVs arrived as replacements over the next few days (KH804 & KH816). The squadron lost two more Mk.IIIs and one Mk.IV (KH803) hit by flak while attacking a train on the 14th. Its pilot (F//Sgt N. Stevenson) was able to return base where he crash-landed. The Mustang was too damaged to be repaired. Later on, Flying Officer Ashley stalled on landing and crashed on the 21st while returning from an armed recce in KH804. He was seriously injured. Five days later another Mk.IV was lost. Early in the afternoon, an offensive sweep carried out on Gornji Stupnik aerodrome consisted of two Mk.IVs (KH816 and KH809 led by F/L William J.P. Straker) and two Mk.IIIs. Straker was taking aim at an Fw190 on the ground when he became aware that Lt. Winston St. C. Thomson (SAAF), his No.2 in KH809 on his starboard wing, had been hit and was engulfed in flames. Straker ordered Thompson on the R/T to pull up and get out but the South African was unable to do so as he was too low. Straker saw him plough straight into the ground. 'Tommy' Thomson, in fact, pulled off the miraculous feat of releasing his straps, whipping off his helmet, jettisoning the canopy, winding the trim fully forward, pushing the stick forward and bunting. He pulled the ripcord as he was flung out and his parachute opened just before he hit the enemy airfield. He was captured but alive! March had proven to be a deadly month for the squadron. About 250 sorties had been carried out, including ninety for the Mk.IVs. However, eight Mustangs had been lost on ops including four brand new and still rare Mk.IVs.

In April, even though combat on the ground was winding down in this part of Europe, the squadron continued to fly every day to harass the German troops retreating to Austria. More than 300 sorties were flown that month and half were flown by Mustang Mk.IVs. That month, the following Mk.IVs were issued to the squadron: KH688, KH748, KH759, KH780, KH782, KH840 and KH869. The aim was of course to replace the war-weary Mk.IIIs within a couple of weeks but this was not achieved. About half of the inventory still consisted of Mark IIIs. Losses, however, were light in April compared to the previous month with two Mk.IIIs and two Mk.IVs being lost to ground fire and one shot down by Enemy fighters. The first Mk.IV loss occurred on return from an armed recce on 16 April. The aircraft, KH780, swung on landing at Prkos in a strong crosswind. The pilot, South African Ian D. Kenyon, attempted an overshoot but stalled, dropped to the ground and cartwheeled. The aircraft was too damaged to consider any repair. The second Mk.IV, KH816, was lost on 23 April while attacking a train during an armed recce over the Zagreb area early in the morning. Flight Sergeant Farley was hit by ground fire and the aircraft was seen to make a safe belly landing before Farley ran through a clearing to nearby woods. Later in the morning, F/L 'Ginger' Husle in KH826/AK-G took off an armed recce leading three other Mk. IVs. By midday they were in the vicinity of Zagreb when they were bounced at 8000 ft by a pair of Croatian Bf109s. Flying

Officer Francis Barrett was hit by fire from the Croatian ace Captain Ljudevit Bencetic and he became his last of his 16 victories. The Croatians attacked from above and behind and Barrett called up to say he had been hit in the prot wingtip. The Bf109s then broke down and Husle attacked one from close range at 2000 ft. He followed the 109 down to the ground and fired several bursts closing to 150 yards, observing 10-15 strikes on its port wing and fuselage. He saw pieces of aircraft breaking away in a cloud of black smoke. Then he ran out of ammunition while he was closed to Zagreb aerodrome. There, Husle reported light flak which probably sealed the fate of Barratt already hit by the 109 and did not returned from this engagement. As for Husle, he could only claim the 109 as damaged, but that became the very last claim made by a Commonwealth fighter pilot in the Mediterranean theatre of operations. Four days later the squadron moved to Prkos in Yugoslavia where the last missions of the war were flown. This move was necessary so as to be closer to the targets the squadron had to neutralise. From Prkos, 39 sorties were flown, twenty of them by Mk.IVs. The last operation was flown on 5 May with F/O Turton E.G. Purchas in KH782 leading three Mk.IIIs on an armed recce over the Logatec-Ljubljana-Celje-Vransko area. Various ground targets were strafed and two direct hits were scored on some wagons. If flak was encountered, it did not damage the aircraft or wound the pilots. The section landed at 09.40 after two hours and fifteen minutes of flight. The squadron moved from Prkos, on 14 May, to Biferno, the western Allies being all but welcomed now in Yugoslavia. The attitude of the partisans had been rather reserved since the arrival of the squadron in the country. What could not be taken was destroyed or burnt such as Mustang KH782 which had been damaged in an accident on the 11th when it swung on landing and hit a Hurricane of the Yugoslavian-manned No. 351 Squadron (KZ723).

The squadron remained in Italy and then moved to Ramat David in Palestine in September. By that time it had been fully equipped with the Mk.IV since August and all of the Dominion personnel (mainly South Africans) had left some time ago. Not all made the move, however, as, on 2 July, F/O O. Wilson-North was killed in his Mustang when it broke up in flight five miles north-east of Ostuni in Italy. It had previously been seen descending with the port wing detached and the two parts fell about three miles apart. It was thought that the pilot was the victim of a structural failure after high negative 'g' had been applied. Another Mustang, KM269, did not make the journey to Palestine either as it was abandoned by its pilot fifteen miles east of Fano after having hit the water when flying at low altitude. The pilot had lost the horizon for a few precious moments and let the aircraft lose height. He was able to recover control, climb to 3,000 feet and bail out. Another Mustang (KM101) was lost on landing on 18 December. The pilot, F/O Wittridge was injured when the aircraft hit the ground after stalling at twenty feet. It cartwheeled and broke up. Post-war restrictions had impacted the amount of training that could be flown and in turn led to a higher accident rate. On 26 June 1946, KH797 was lost during an army liaison exercise. The Mustang swung on landing at RAF Deversoir and went off the side of the runway into soft sand before tipping over on to its back. Less than one month later, the pilot of KH831 forgot to lower the undercarriage and made a belly landing at Heliopolis. Of course the propeller and underside of the aircraft were both damaged, and the aircraft found repairable, but with the impending withdrawal of the type, and the number of brand new Mk.IVs still on charge, the Mustang was not repaired and struck off charge. Then, on 6 September, F/L Eric J. Holman in KM214 undershot his approach and stalled into the ground thirty yards short of the runway where he bounced and overturned. The cause of the accident was attributed to a number of factors. Norman had only flown the Mk.IV fifteen times previously and had a deformity in his right arm, caused by a previous accident, that prevented him from making a full recovery when the Mustang bounced. Two weeks later, it was the turn of KM111. The pilot failed to put his undercarriage control lever to the full down position so the undercarriage was, therefore, not locked down. Consequently, it collapsed on landing and, despite being repairable, the fate of KM111 followed KH831 as it was so close to the end the Mustang IV's career with the RAF. In October 1946 the squadron moved once more to Nicosia in Cyprus. The Mustangs would continue to fly with the squadron until February 1947 when they were replaced by Tempest Mk.VIs.

By the spring of 1945 many of the Mustang IVs of No. 213 Squadron were not camouflaged. Here are KH797/AK-A and KH826/AK-G which was flown by F/L Husle in the final air combat in the Med. Note the squadron codes, painted on the same side of the roundel. This was typical of 213 Sqn's Mustangs.
(via Andrew Thomas)

Summary of the aircraft lost on Operations - 213 Squadron

Date	Pilot	S/N	Origin	Serial	Code	Fate
01.03.45	F/O Arthur G.R. **ASHLEY**	RAF No. 146133	RAF	**KH823**		-
02.03.45	F/O Peter **DONNELLY**	RAF No. 162166	RAF	**KH846**		**PoW**
11.03.45	W/O Ian R.H. **IAGO**	RAF No. 1795095	RAF	**KH693**		†
14.03.45	F/Sgt Norman **STEVENSON**	RAF No. 1545772	RAF	**KH803**	AK-J	-
21.03.45	F/O Arthur G.R. **ASHLEY**	RAF No. 146133	RAF	**KH804**		Inj.
24.03.45	Lt Winston St. C. **THOMSON**	SAAF No. 543150	SAAF	**KH809**		**PoW**
16.04.45	Lt Ian D. **KENYON**	SAAF No. 581628	SAAF	**KH780**		-
23.04.45	F/Sgt Sidney W. **FARLEY**	RAF No. 1585005	RAF	**KH816**		**PoW**
	F/L Francis J. **BARRETT**	RAF No. 151845	RAF	**KH869**		†

Total: **9**

Left, the New-Zealander Don Robertson posing in front of the wing of one 213 Sqn's Mustang IVs, KH861. His war did not end quietly as he was shot down by flak on 20 April while flying a Mk. III (HB853). He managed to evade capture and returned to the squadron on 11 May.
(D.E Robertson via Paul Sortehaug)

Summary of the aircraft lost by accident - 213 Squadron

Date	Pilot	S/N	Origin	Serial	Code	Fate
11.05.45	F/O Turton E.G. **PURCHAS**	RAF No. 146709	RAF	**KH782**		-
02.07.45	F/O Oscar **WILSON-NORTH**	RAF No. 163152	RAF	**KM116**		†
31.07.45	Sgt James I.T. **WILLIAMSON**	RAF No. 546595	RAF	**KM262**		-
18.12.45	F/O Arthur H. **WITTRIDGE**	RAF No. 133104	RAF	**KM101**		-
26.06.46	F/O Arthur G. **SMITH**	RAF No. 193136	RAF	**KH797**		-
19.07.46	F/Sgt Hugh T. **MARTIN**	RAF No. 1570175	RAF	**KH831**		-
06.09.46	F/L Eric J. **HOLMAN**	RAF No. 125518	RAF	**KM214**		-
20.09.46	F/Sgt Herbert **MARSHAL**	RAF No. 1588422	RAF	**KM111**		-

Total: **8**

Mustang IV KM348 seen at Nicosia (Cyprus) in 1947.

WITH THE OTHER FIGHTER SQUADRONS

When the war ended in the region, various fighter units operating over the Balkans or over Italy were scheduled to convert to the Mustang IV (occasionally supplemented by Mk. IIIs).

No. 93 Squadron, code DV:
A Spitfire unit fighting in the Mediterranean since the end of 1942, the squadron disbanded in Austria in September 1945. It reformed on 1 January 1946 when No. 237 (Rhodesia) Squadron was re-numbered. At that time, 237 had just begun to exchange its Spitfires for Mustangs so the new 93 would continue to use 237's 'DV' squadron codes instead of its wartime 'HN'. The squadron was stationed at Lavariano and Treviso in Italy until 30 December when it disbanded once more. Not that much is known about the aircraft used but among the known Mk. IVs is KH798 which was lost in an accident at Treviso on 17 June 1946. After take off, the aircraft climbed to a height of 1,200 feet to join up with others from the unit. While doing so the Mustang stalled and entered a spin from which it did not recover before striking the ground. The pilot, Flight Sergeant Thomas A. Every was killed. Other Mk. IVs known to have flown with the squadron were KH727/DV-J, KH799, KM110/DV-Z and KM131 (possibly DV-R).

Summary of the aircraft lost by accident - 93 Squadron

Date	Pilot	S/N	Origin	Serial	Code	Fate
17.06.46	F/Sgt Thomas A. **EVERY**	RAF No. 1617506	RAF	**KH798**		†
		Total: 1				

Four Mustang IVs of 93 Sqn, with another from 112 Sqn, flying over the Alps. The codes are DV-R, DV-X, DV-W and DV-Z.

Two Mustang IVs of 93 Sqn in 1946. Left, KH727/DV-J and, right, DV-M which cannot be identified. Note that the anti-glare panel and hood are yellow. The placement of the serial is also, typical of a Mustang in service in the UK. Indeed, this aircraft was first shipped to the UK before being sent to the Mediterranean. Below, DV-S and DV-Y in flight. *(Andrew Thomas)*

No. 249 (Gold Coast) Squadron, code GN:

The squadron operated Mustangs IIIs from September 1944. However, in April 1945, due to a critical shortage of Mustangs elsewhere, the squadron, while based at Pkros in Yugoslavia, handed over most of its remaining aircraft to 213 Squadron and re-equipped with Spitfires until the end of war. When hostilities came to an end in Europe, the squadron returned to Biferno, Italy, to convert back to Mustangs, and immediately took on a handful of Mk. IVs. The process was slow and the squadron used both Spitfires and Mustangs during May and June. In June, KH835 was recorded as being part of the squadron's strength as it flew a test flight on the 5th. The records also list KH682, KH718, KH757, KH762, KH811, KH870, KM144, KM231, KM247, KM258, KM268 and KM293. By July, all of the Spitfires were gone and, if we ignore the use of two Mustang IIIs in July and August (HB948 & KH424), 249 was actually a Mustang IV squadron when it disbanded on 16 August 1945. Earlier that month, the squadron received another Mk. IV, KH803, which only flew once wearing 'GN' codes.

Mustang IV KH682/GN-B was issued to No. 249 Squadron with the code GN-B. Note how the code was painted ahead of the fuselage roundel and that the fuselage band has not been painted out. This Mustang was sent to Italy after VE-Day and belonged to a batch first sent to the UK.

No. 250 (Sudan) Squadron, code LD:

A Kittyhawk squadron until the end of war, 250 switched to the Mustang in August 1945 when No. 260 Squadron disbanded and handed its Mustangs over. At that time 260 only had three Mustang Mk. IVs on strength (KH773, KH854 and KM249). No. 250 Squadron would remain a Mustang squadron until it was disbanded on 30 December 1946.

No. 260 Squadron, code HS:

After many years flying Curtiss Kittyhawks, No. 260 Squadron converted to the Mustang in April 1944. Until the war's end, however, it continued to fly Mk. IIIs with one exception. KH705 was issued to the squadron at the end of November 1944. This Mustang made its operational debut with Capt Roy T. Rogers (SAAF) on 3 December on an armed reconnaissance around Sarajevo in Yugoslavia. It was used until the end of February and then passed to No. 5 Squadron, SAAF. After the end of hostilities, three more Mk. IVs were issued to 260 (KH773, KH854 and KM249) but were passed to No. 250 Squadron when 260 disbanded.

No. 450 (RAAF) Squadron, code OK:

When the war ended in Italy, the squadron was about to exchange its Kittyhawk Mk. IVs for Mustangs. This process seems to have been stopped early and never completed as the squadron, like other Australian units located in Italy or the Mediterranean, was intended for disbandment or, at least, the majority of its personnel repatriated. The number of Mustangs issued to the squadron is uncertain but about half a dozen are clearly identified and included one Mk. IV (KM250/OK-R). The squadron therefore flew Mk. IIIs and the Mk. IV until disbandment on 24 August 1945. Whatever the number, the hours flown were low as daily work concentrated on preparing personnel for repatriation. All of the aircraft were handed over to No. 380 MU aircraft storage unit at Campoformido.

Mustang IVA KM250, an aircraft sent from the UK after VE-Day, was issued to the Australian squadron during the summer of 194, and eventually found its way to No. 112 Squadron. This aircraft was struck off charge in March 1946, an early withdrawal compared to the entire fleet. The RAF, with the end of Lend-Lease in September 1945, had to pay cash for the spare parts so, to avoid this, used many Mustangs on hand to provide parts for the airworthy airframes. Also, the RAF did not carry out any major repairs or overhauls to save costs. The aircraft selected for this purpose were usually slightly damaged or in need of an overhaul. This was possible as the Americans, having so many in their depots, did not ask for the Mustangs to be returned as they didn't need the RAF aircraft. *(AHW of WA)*

WITH THE SECOND LINE UNITS

A lack of records, generally destroyed at the end of the war, prevent the formulation of a clear idea of the usage of the Mustang IV in the Middle East. From other sources, like pilot's logbooks, it is known that some Mustangs were issued to No. 71 OTU based at Ismaïlia in Egypt. This operational training was responsible, by 1945, for training fighter pilots on various types of fighters operated first by the Desert Air Force and then by the Balkan Air Force. With the end of the war in Europe, flying training was suspended on 20 May and the OTU disbanded on 11 June. It is known that KH837, KH842, KM109, KM117 and KM119 were used by No. 71 out. KH837 was lost in a fatal accident on 18 April 1945 when the pilot, Sgt Herbert A. Cooper, lost control at 25,000 feet, possibly due to an oxygen failure, and dived into the ground. It is worth noting that, as far as we know from the existing records of all kind, only the Mustang Mk. IV was issued to OTU in the Middle East. The reason is that the Mk. III had been always in short supply for the operational squadrons in Italy so there were no spare aircraft for the OTUs while the numbers of Mustang IVs arriving in the region was growing month by month.

In the same vein, No. 1330 Conversion Unit (CU) received some Mustangs (one known, KH849), to give conversion training to crews transferred to new types, while No. 5 Refresher Flying Unit (RFU) was established in July 1944 to provide additional flying experience on the operational types used in the Mediterranean. Three Mk. IVs are known to have been flown by 5 RFU (KH792, KH815 and KM856) alongside a few Mk. IIIs (5 RFU had an establishment of five Mustangs). As with 71 OTU, disbandment came quickly, after the end of the hostilities, in August 1945.

Otherwise, logically, many Ferry Units were involved in ferrying Mustangs to various places in the Middle East, during and after the war and some never reached their destination. A list of such accidents is included below with the other known Mustang IV accidents. As in the UK, when the British types became available, the Mustang eventually disappeared from the RAF's inventory and the last examples had been struck off charge by the end of 1947.

Date	Pilot	S/N	Origin	Serial	Code	Unit	Fate
21.11.44	F/O MacNamara R. DOOLEY	CAN./ J.17871	RCAF	KH699		3 FU	-
15.01.45	F/L Stanislaw SWIECHOWSKI	PAF P-0206	PAF	KH801		3 FU	†
02.03.45	F/Sgt Henry E. BANGS	RAF No. 1331408	RAF	KH827		4 FU	-
14.04.45	F/Sgt Denis CLARKE	RAF No. 1581840	RAF	KM133		159 MU	-
23.03.45	F/O Bruce J. DUMBRELL	AUS. 409396	RAAF	KH733		12 FU	-
18.04.45	Sgt Herbert A. COOPER	RAF No. 1812582	RAF	KH837		71 OTU	†
01.08.45	Ground accident	-	-	KM535		3 FP	-
05.08.45	P/O Herbert W. THOMAS	RAF No. 190203	RAF	KM415		15 FU	-
19.08.45	F/L Gerald C.D. GREEN	RAF No. 103594	RAF	KM622		158 SP	†
	W/O Denys MITCHELL	RAF No. 1338666	RAF	KM631		158 SP	†
15.11.45	F/O Noel J. DE VERTEUIL*	RAF No. 170477	RAF	KM723		36 SP	-
20.02.46	F/O Michael V. FRANCIS	RAF No.191448	RAF	KM354		17 SP	-

*From Trinidad

Some Mustang IVs, like KM182, became the personal mount of high-ranking officers. This was G/C Donald R. Shore's aircraft. He was the OC of No. 239 Wing comprising, just before disbandment in January 1947, Nos. 93, 112 and 250 Squadrons (all Mustang units). During the war Ross had served as an anti-shipping pilot on Beaufighters in the Mediterranean.

Brian Alexander EATON
AUS. 133

Brian Eaton was an Australian from Tasmania who enlisted in the RAAF in January 1936. By the outbreak of the war he was serving as a flying instructor. He remained in Australia until October 1942 when he sailed for North Africa and joined 3 Sqn, flying Kittyhawks, in January 1943 as a flight commander. Four months later he took over the unit and led it until March 1944 when he was rested, having been awarded a DFC in the meantime, and was made Companion of the DSO in April 1944 for his leadership. In August 1944, he returned to operational flying duty by taking command, as a group captain, of 239 Wing, replacing Lt-Col Wilmot. He led the wing until the end of the war and added a Bar to his DSO in June 1945. He remained in the RAAF, reaching the rank of Air-Vice Marshal, until retiring in December 1973.

North American Mustang Mk. IVA KH745
No. 239 Wing
Group Captain B.A. Eaton
Cervia (Italy), April 1945

In January 1946, 'Jas' Storrar selected Mustang IV KM264 as his personal mount while serving at the head of 239 Wing in Italy. Above, Group Captain Eaton leading in his mount, KH745.

James Eric STORRAR
RAF No. 41881

'Jas' Storrar joined the RAF on a Short Service Commission in October 1938. On completion of his training in August 1939, he was destined to fly Blenheims with No. 145 Squadron when he finally reached the unit in October. In May, the squadron converted to Hurricanes just in time to participate in the air combats over Dunkirk. Between 23 and 27 May, he claimed no less than four German aircraft destroyed and his tally continued to increase considerably during the Battle of Britain with ten more claims which, naturally, led to the award of a DFC in August. In September, he was posted to No. 73 Squadron with which he sailed to Africa in November. Attached initially to No. 274 Squadron, 73 eventually began to fight on its own account from January 1941. Storrar had made five more claims by April when he was sent for a rest period ferrying aircraft. He returned to the UK in November and served with No. 55 OTU until January 1943 after which he returned to operations as OC of No. 65 (East India) Squadron flying Spitfires. With this unit he would make his final claims, the last, a Fw190 destroyed, on 18 September to bring his total to fourteen confirmed victories (two shared), four unconfirmed or probably destroyed (one shared) and three aircraft damaged. The following month, he added a Bar to his DFC and was posted out for a rest in November. He started a third tour of operations in October 1944 as a supernumerary squadron leader with No. 64 Squadron for about two months before he was given command of No. 165 (Ceylon) Squadron, between November 1944 and January 1945, and No. 234 Squadron between January and March 1945. Both units were equipped with the Mustang III. In April 1945, he was briefly WingCo Flying of the Hundson Wing and held the same position with the Digby Wing (May - July) and the Molesworth Wing (July - August). In January 1946 he went out to Italy to lead No. 239 Wing, on Mustangs once more. He left the RAF in April 1947, but would serve with the RAuxAF between June 1949 and March 1957.

North American Mustang Mk. IVA KM264
No. 239 Wing
Wing Commander JE Storrar
Tissano (Italy), spring 1946

IN THE FAR EAST

The Mustang was also destined to operate in the Far East and 225 of them were shipped directly to India where they were uncrated. They were intended to replace the Thunderbolts in eight squadrons but the uncrating was still underway when Japan surrendered. Only a handful were made airworthy and sent to 1331 CU to start conversion courses. The first Mustang did not arrive before the end of August and the conversion course began in September. Only three pilots were actually converted, representing less than ten hours of flight, before the process was halted when it was decided that the Thunderbolt would continue to serve until it was replaced by a British-made type. This was possible because the RAF had many Thunderbolts in storage and, therefore, enough to provide spare parts to keep the squadrons flying. This was essential as the Lend Lease Act terminated in September 1945. Indeed, it would have been totally uneconomical to convert the Thunderbolt squadrons onto the Mustang, knowing that the Mustang also to be replaced by a British-made aircraft as soon as possible. Mustangs known to have been issued to No. 1331 CU are KM557, KM562, KM584, KM590, KM591, KM595, KM597 and KM639. At least two found also their way to TWDU (Tactical &Weapons Development Unit) stationed at Armada Road. Both (KM147 and KM174) were lost in accidents which is why there is some trace of them with this unit. KM147 was lost on 4 June 1945 when the engine failed on take off at fifty feet. The pilot escaped major injuries. KM174 was the victim of the same kind of accident on 27 July. The cause of KM174's engine failure was never clearly identified but faulty plugs were found to be the cause of KM147's demise.

With VJ-Day, the Mustang didn't get the opportunity to fill the role the RAF had reserved for it and most of the Mustangs dispatched to the Far East were stored (and possibly some were never uncrated) and were massively struck off charge between March and July 1946. Remembering that the Australians, the New Zealanders and even the Dutch were also in the process of fully re-equipping with Mustangs, a continuing war against Japan would have been a major chapter in the Mustang's Commonwealth story.

Date	Pilot	S/N	Origin	Serial	Code	Unit	Fate
04.06.45	F/L Arthur E. LEE	RAF No. 42981	RAF	**KM147**		T&WDU	-
27.07.45	S/L John F.D. ELKINGTON	RAF No. 44184	RAF	**KM174**		T&WDU	-

Mustang IV KM545 being refueled at an MU in the Far East. This Mustang was SOC on 25 April 1946. *(Phil Butler)*

Mustang IVA KM735 was one of the last taken on charge by the RAF and shipped to the Far East. At that time, all the American aircraft were left in a natural metal finish and were issued to the squadrons like this. This Mustang was ready to receive its squadron and tactical codes but this never happened and KM735 was SOC on April 25 1946. *(Phil Butler)*

North American Mustang Mk. IVA KH760
No. 3 Squadron, RAAF
Cervia (Italy), April 1945

North American Mustang Mk. IV KH671
No. 5 Squadron, SAAF
Lavariano (Italy), May 1945
N.B.: The roundels are shown here before being overpainted in orange

North American Mustang Mk. IVA KH741
No. 5 Squadron, SAAF
Cervia (Italy), April 1945

SQUADRONS! - The series

Donald James Matthew BLAKESLEE DFC
Supermarine Spitfire Mk.VB EN951
No. 133 (Eagle) Squadron
Flight Lieutenant D. J. M. Blakeslee
CAN./ J-4351
Gravesend (UK), August 1942

Charles Cuthbertson LEARMONTH DFC*
Douglas Boston Mk. III A28-9 (ex-AL810)
No. 22 Squadron RAAF
Squadron Leader C. C. Learmonth
Aus. 385
Port Moresby (New Guinea), spring 1943

Hans Anton MAURENBRECHER
Curtiss P-40N-35-CU C3-560
No. 120 (NEI) Squadron
Majoor H. Maurenbrecher
Biak (New Guinea), 1943-1946

Roland Prosper BEAMONT DSO* DFC*
Hawker Tempest Mk V JN751
No. 150 Wing
Wing Commander R. P. Beamont
RAF No. 40819
Bradwell Bay (UK), April 1944

Ronald Thomas SUSANS DSO DFC
North American P-51D-25-NT A68-724
No. 77 Squadron, RAAF
Squadron Leader R. T. Susans
O4391
Bofu (Japan), 1947

James Henry LACEY DFM*
Supermarine Spitfire Mk.XIV RN135
No. 17 Squadron
Squadron Leader J. H. Lacey
RAF No. 117708
Seletar (Singapore), autumn 1945

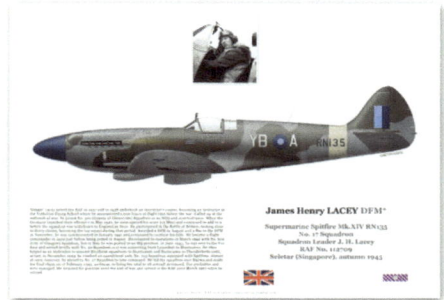

Introducing's RAF In Combat and Bravo Bravo Aviation's collection of
highly-detailed and historically accurate, high-quality aviation prints.
For more information on available prints, please visit :

www.RAF-IN-COMBAT.com   or   BRAVO BRAVO AVIATION
BBA
HIGH QUALITY AVIATION ILLUSTRATION
WWW.BRAVOBRAVOAVIATION.COM

Hendrick Oswald Meyer ODENDAAL DFC*
North American Mustang Mk. IVA KH805
No. 5 Squadron, SAAF
Captain H. O. M. Odendaal
SAAF No. 103164
Cervia (Italy), March 1945

Prints in connection with the book:

PL-078: HOM Odendaal
PL-104: J.E. Storrar
PL-238: M.P. Nash
PL-239: HOM Odendaal (2)
PL-240: H.J.E. Clarke
PL-241: J.S. Hart
PL-242: P.E. Vaughan-Fowler
PL-243: B.A. Eaton

www.ingramcontent.com/pod-product-compliance
Lightning Source LLC
Chambersburg PA
CBHW042011080426

42734CB00002B/45